Weather

Deborah Chancellor

KINGFISHER

NEW YORK

KINGFISHER
LONDON & NEW YORK

Copyright © Kingfisher 2010
Published in the United States by Kingfisher,
175 Fifth Ave., New York, NY 10010
Kingfisher is an imprint of Macmillan Children's Books, London.

Illustrations by Peter Bull Art Studio

Distributed in the U.S. by Macmillan, 175 Fifth Ave.,
New York, NY 10010
Distributed in Canada by H.B. Fenn and Company Ltd.,
34 Nixon Road, Bolton, Ontario L7E 1W2

Library of Congress Cataloging-in-Publication data
has been applied for.

ISBN: 978-0-7534-6421-2

Kingfisher books are available for special promotions and
premiums. For details contact: Special Markets Department,
Macmillan, 175 Fifth Ave., New York, NY 10010.

For more information, please visit
www.kingfisherpublications.com

Printed in China
1 3 5 7 9 8 6 4 2
1TR/0410/WKT/UNTD/140MA

Picture credits

**The Publisher would like to thank the following
for permission to reproduce their images
(t = top, b = bottom, c = center, r = right, l = left):**
Cover (sky and raindrops) Shutterstock/Vjom; Pages 4bl
Shutterstock/Morgan Lane Photography; 4c Getty/Taxi/Guy
Edwardes; 4br Shutterstock/Greg Randles; 5tl Alamy/Image Source
Pink; 5tr Corbis/Weatherstock; 5b Photolibrary/Jean-Louis Batt;
6tl Science Photo Library (SPL)/John Beatty; 8bl SPL/SFR;
8tr SPL/Martyn F. Chillmaid; 8br SPL/Garry D. McMichael;
9tl iStockphoto; 9bl Corbis/Kurt Kormann; 9br Alamy/Image Source
Pink; 10tl Shutterstock/Petr Vaclavek; 12c NHPA/Jordi Bas Casas;
12bc Shutterstock/Anton Foltin; 12cr Shutterstock/Ricardo Miguel;
13tl Arcticphoto; 13tr Shutterstock/Ragnarok; 13bl Shutterstock/
Sascha Burkard; 13br Photolibrary/Corbis; 14tl Shutterstock/Carlos
Caetano; 16bl FLPA/ImageBroker; 16br Photolibrary/Dennis Hallinan;
17tl FLPA/ImageBroker; 17tr FLPA/ImageBroker 17cl Shutterstock/
Wolfgang Zintl; 17cr Alamy/Lou Linwei; 17b Shutterstock/Can
Balcioglu; 18bl Shutterstock/carroteater; 20cl Alamy/RHPL;
20bl Shutterstock/NatalieJean; 21tl Corbis/Mick Tsikas;
21r Shutterstock/Monkey Business Images; 21br Alamy/Ian
Woolcock; 22bl Shutterstock/James Steidl; 24bl Getty/ Martin Puddy;
24r all SPL/Kenneth Libbrecht; 24br Shutterstock/Petr Masek;
25tc Alamy/Mike Lane; 25tl Corbis/Jim Reed; 25r Shutterstock/
Ilja Masik; 26tl Corbis/Gavin Hellier/RHPL; 28b Photolibrary/Sven-Erik
Arndt; 28cr Shutterstock/kwest; 29tr Shutterstock/Markus Gann;
29cl Corbis/Tibor Bognr; 29br Alamy/Steven May;
30tl Shutterstock/Alexandro; 30tc Shutterstock/Christi Matei;
30cr Alamy/Nigel Hicks; 31tr Shutterstock/Leksele; 31cr Alamy/Ryan
McGinnis; 31cr Shutterstock/S. Borisov.

Contents

Choose your own journey

On some of the pages in this book, you will find colored buttons with symbols on them. There are four different colors of buttons, and each belongs to a journey you can follow. Choose a journey, follow it through the book, and you'll make some interesting discoveries of your own.

For example, on page 6 you'll find a blue button next to a weather scientist at the South Pole, like this:

Page 26

People

There is a page number in the button. Turn to that page (26) to find the next step of the journey. All the steps in this journey have something to do with the topic of people and the weather. Follow the steps through the book, and at the end you'll find out how they are linked and discover extra information about this topic.

Science

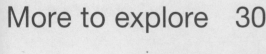

Environment

Animals

The other journeys in this book are science, environment, and animals. Follow a journey and see what you can discover!

What is weather?

What is the weather like where you are today? There are many types of weather. The weather is always changing, affecting what you can do and what you need to wear. Patterns of weather are different, too, depending on where in the world you live.

Snow falls when ice crystals in clouds join together to make snowflakes. Snow is great for building snowpeople, but when the weather warms up again, they melt away.

Fog makes it hard to see anything very far ahead.

Lighthouse sends out beams of light.

snowman

wind turbines

In sunny weather, you need protection from the Sun's rays.

Clouds are made of tiny water droplets or ice crystals. There are many kinds of clouds— some bring rain, and some bring snow.

tall rain cloud

Wind power is used by wind turbines to create electricity. Wind is made when the Sun warms the air, making it rise. Cooler air moves in to fill the gap. Strong winds often bring storms.

Puddles are made by the rain. They are fun to jump in! Rain happens when drops of water in the clouds join together. They form bigger, heavier drops that fall to the ground as rain.

Rubber boots keep your feet dry in wet weather.

1. marker at the South Pole
2. Amundsen-Scott weather station
3. weather plane

What is this?

Page 26

Weather station

The science of studying weather is called meteorology, and weather scientists are called meteorologists. Some scientists work at weather stations like this one. Others study data that has been collected at sea on weather ships, in the air by planes, and in space by satellites.

Page 14

Scientists measure weather conditions everywhere, even in the most extreme climates. Antarctica, the coldest and windiest continent, is home to several weather stations. Meteorologists travel to Antarctica from all over the world to record the weather. They use tough instruments that can withstand the cold.

This is an anemometer. It is an instrument that is used to measure wind speed.

Weather watching

Every day, all over the world, meteorologists use special instruments to record changes in the weather. This information helps them make weather forecasts, so that we know what kind of weather we are going to have in the near future.

anemometer

weather-vane

thermometer

Shelters contain all the instruments that are needed to keep track of the weather. People take measurements at the same time every day of the year, whatever the weather.

Weather instruments include weathervanes and anemometers to measure wind direction and speed. Thermometers show the temperature of the air.

A scientist writes down the day's measurements.

Rain gauges measure how much rain has fallen in a particular place. Information about past rainfall helps weather watchers predict how much rain might fall in the future.

rain gauge

Falling air pressure means that rain is on the way.

Barometers measure air pressure—the force of air pressing down on the Earth. When air pressure rises or falls, the weather changes.

Weather houses work by using changes in the amount of water— or humidity—in the air. If the air is damp, the man moves out of the house. If the air is dry, the woman comes out. This weather house also has a thermometer.

weather satellite

Satellites orbit Earth to collect weather data. They send information back to Earth to be studied, so meteorologists can forecast the weather. Satellite images are used to predict and track violent storms.

Solar panels generate electricity for the satellite.

Marks and symbols on weather maps stand for different kinds of weather.

TV meteorologists use maps to tell us about the weather.

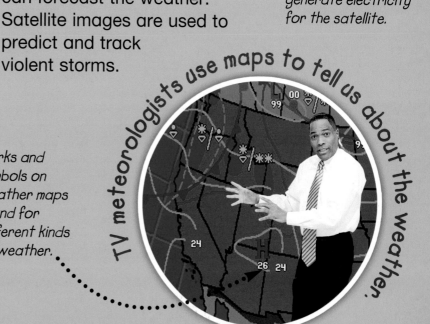

1 Many leaves change color in the fall.

2 Deciduous trees lose their leaves.

3 puddles from autumn rain

What is this?

Page 30

Page 27

The four seasons

In many parts of the world, there are four seasons: spring, summer, fall (autumn), and winter. After the cool spring comes the hot summer, and the windy, rainy fall is followed by the cold winter. Then the cycle of seasons begins all over again.

4

Page 19

Many leaves change color and drop from the trees in the fall. Fallen leaves are fun to kick around! There is more rain now than in the spring and summer and the weather is colder, so people wrap up warmly. There are also fewer hours of daylight.

5

6

These are acorns. Acorns fall from oak trees. Some take root and grow into new oak trees.

Different climates

Climate is the pattern of weather over a period of time. Different parts of the world have different climates. For example, rainforests have rain all year round, but deserts hardly have any rain. At the North and South poles, the ice never melts.

In mild climates, **spring** is the season of new life. Animals have babies, trees grow leaves, and seeds begin to grow in the soil.

mother swallow bringing food

swallow chicks in the spring

Deserts are very dry—few living things survive in this climate.

Plants are good at adapting to the climate. The cactus is a desert plant. In the desert, it hardly ever rains, but when it does, the cactus soaks up water to store in its thick stem.

saguaro cactus

Fur clothes keep Inuit children warm in the freezing cold.

Inuit people live in a cold, polar climate. They have found ways of surviving the long, icy winters of the Arctic. People and animals must adapt to the climate where they live.

rainforest tree frog

The rainforest climate is very hot and wet. Frogs usually live in water, but rainforest frogs can survive high up in the trees because the air is so damp.

Places near the equator (red line) have a hot climate.

Climates can be warm, cool, or cold, depending on how far away from the equator you live. The equator is an imaginary line around the middle of the world.

Summer brings hot weather. When it is summer in the northern half of the world, it is winter in the southern half.

cooling ice cream—yum!

What is this?

① low-level nimbostratus cloud

② low-level cumulus cloud

③ mid-level stratocumulus cloud

④

Page 19

Page 22

Page 27

Cloud watching

Earth is surrounded by a layer of gases that we call the atmosphere. Clouds are in the lowest part of the atmosphere, which is called the troposphere. They form at different heights and come in many shapes and sizes.

Low-level clouds, made of water droplets, form up to 1 mi. (2km) above the ground. Between 1 and 4 mi. (2 and 6km) above ground, water droplets and ice crystals mix together in mid-level clouds. High-level clouds, packed with ice crystals, float more than 4 mi. (6km) above our heads.

Baskets under hot-air balloons carry passengers high up into the sky.

Clouds and fog

When warm air rises and cools, clouds are made from millions of little water droplets or ice crystals. Not all clouds in the sky lead to changes in the weather, but many of them bring rain, snow, or hail.

The white, puffy tops of cumulonimbus clouds are lit up by sunshine.

An umbrella keeps you dry.

Cumulonimbus clouds stretch up through all levels of the troposphere. They can cover an area about 3 mi. (5km) wide and grow taller than Mount Everest, the world's highest mountain!

sea fog at the Golden Gate Bridge, San Francisco, California

nimbostratus cloud

Nimbostratus clouds carry heavy rain or snow. These thick, gray clouds hide the Sun and bring days of bad weather. They often cause floods or deep snowdrifts on the ground.

Cirrostratus clouds warn that snow is on the way.

Snow clouds, such as cirrostratus, are often seen before a snowstorm. They may form a thin layer over the whole sky, like a blanket.

Ice crystals form in the highest clouds in the sky.

Smog is a mix of smoke and fog.

Fog is a low-lying cloud that forms when warm, damp air moves over cold land or sea. When the warm air cools, clouds of water vapor gather near the ground.

Wearing a mask keeps you from breathing in smoggy pollution.

Tornado alert!

Tornadoes are powerful, dangerous windstorms. They can race more than 60 mi. (100km) along the ground, with wind speeds over 300 mph (480km/h). A tornado will destroy everything in its path. Houses and cars are not safe, so people must run to a shelter.

Page 30

What is this?

1 mobile weather station

2 tracking the storm on a computer screen

3 storm chaser

? This is a siren. It warns when a tornado is coming, so people have time to take shelter.

Page 30

5

Tornadoes form when hot air rises quickly. Cool air rushes in from all directions, spinning the hot air around in a storm cloud. A twisting spiral of wind drops down from the storm cloud and sweeps over the ground below. As the swirling funnel sucks up more and more wreckage and dust, it turns dark gray.

6

Page 14

4 Satellite dish sends and receives data.

5 tornado funnel

6 storm shelter

Wind and storms

Some winds are much faster and stronger than others and may turn into windstorms. Hurricanes, typhoons, and cyclones are all the same kind of tropical windstorm, but they happen in different parts of the world.

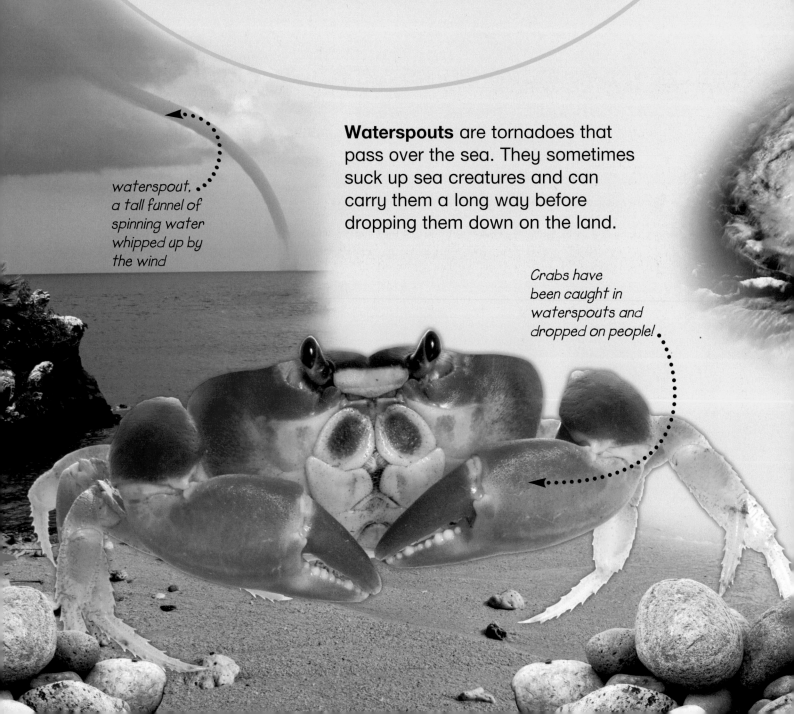

waterspout, a tall funnel of spinning water whipped up by the wind

Waterspouts are tornadoes that pass over the sea. They sometimes suck up sea creatures and can carry them a long way before dropping them down on the land.

Crabs have been caught in waterspouts and dropped on people!

Wildfires destroy large areas of forest in hot, dry weather.

Winds fan the flames, spreading the fire.

The kite is lifted up by the wind.

satellite picture of a hurricane

Kites fly well on a windy day. Meteorologists measure wind strength on the "Beaufort scale." Force 0 is complete calm, Force 5 is a kite-flying breeze, Force 10 is a storm, and Force 12 is a hurricane.

The calm eye in the middle of the storm.

Hurricanes sweep across the sea, causing damage when they hit land. Hurricane winds can reach more than 155 mph (250km/h).

weathervane

Weathervanes point to where the wind is coming from. Winds can blow from any direction between north, south, east, or west.

Rain and snow

Water is always being recycled in a natural process called the water cycle. Rain falls from clouds into rivers and is carried out to sea. When the Sun heats the sea, water vapor rises into the sky. Clouds form again, so rain falls once more into rivers.

Page 10

In this busy city, people are bustling around in warm, waterproof clothes that keep out the cold and wet. Rain is falling now, but there is snow and slush on the ground. Snow falls when the temperature drops below freezing, making water droplets in the clouds turn to ice.

What is this?

Page 18

① Snow settles on mountains.

② A rainbow appears if the Sun shines when it rains.

③ rain turning the snow to slush

? Ice crystals join together in clouds to make beautiful snowflakes like this one.

4

5

6

4 Rain and snowflakes fall from the clouds.

5 Water droplets and ice crystals form in clouds.

6 snow on the ground

Water and ice

Water that falls to Earth from clouds is called precipitation, and it provides us with fresh water to drink. It falls in different forms, either as liquid rain or as frozen snow or hail. Sleet is a mixture of rain and snow.

Monsoon winds bring heavy rain.

The rainy season is one of two seasons in the tropics. Summer is the rainy season, and winter is the dry season. People are glad when the rain arrives. It cools the air and waters the crops.

Lightning strikes when electricity is released from storm clouds.

The arctic fox's fur turns white in the winter.

Animals must adapt in order to survive in snowy places. In the Arctic, many animals and birds are white. This gives them camouflage in the snow.

arctic fox

Hailstones are lumps of ice that form in clouds.

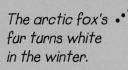

Skiwear keeps out water, the cold, and wind.

Snowflakes are crystals of ice. All snowflakes have six sides, but no two snowflakes are exactly the same.

Snow falls in high places, such as mountains. In the winter, when the temperature drops, snow also falls on lower ground. It is snowy at the North and South poles all year round.

What is this?

① beehive

② Ants carry their eggs to safety.

③ birds returning to the valley after the storm

⑤ Page 22

Changing weather

Weather patterns are changing around the world, and tropical storms are happening more often. Cyclones are tropical storms that bring strong winds and heavy rains to parts of Southeast Asia and Australia. They can cause natural disasters, such as floods.

These elephants have found safety on high ground after a cyclone flooded their valley. Down below, people's stilt houses are just clear of the floodwater. Animals and people must adapt to survive tropical storms and other extreme weather.

Page 14

6

Page 30

Stilt houses like these are built in some tropical countries, where rivers often flood.

Weather in the future

Around the world, temperatures are slowly rising. This change in Earth's climate is called global warming. Many countries now have warmer winters, earlier springs, and wetter summers. Pollution is beginning to affect our patterns of weather.

Droughts happen when there is not enough rain.

polar bear

Melting Arctic ice is making sea levels rise.

In the Arctic, warmer winters are melting the ice faster than ever before. This is bad for Arctic animals, like the polar bear.

the Sun

solar panels on a roof

Harmful gases trap the Sun's rays so that heat can't escape from Earth's atmosphere. This causes the problem of global warming.

Solar panels soak up the Sun's energy and change it into electricity. This is one way we make "clean" power from the weather.

Cities use up lots of energy and create pollution.

Traffic releases harmful gases into the atmosphere.

Riding a bike is one way to help cut traffic pollution, which is a cause of global warming. Walking or using buses and trains also helps.

Cycling is good for you and the environment.

Animals

Many animals migrate between different climates. In the fall, **swallows** in northern Europe prepare to fly to southern Africa to spend the winter.

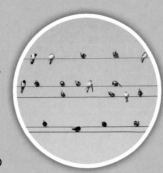

Some animals can sense that a storm is coming long before it actually strikes. **Pets** may behave strangely—for example, dogs may start to bark or try to hide.

People

Meteorologists are weather experts. They use instruments and machines to collect data about the weather and then use computers to study it. You can measure the weather, too.

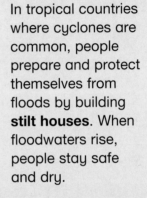

In tropical countries where cyclones are common, people prepare and protect themselves from floods by building **stilt houses**. When floodwaters rise, people stay safe and dry.

Science

weather balloon

Weather balloons are released from weather stations twice a day. They carry radiosondes, which measure temperature, humidity, and pressure at different heights in the sky.

When air gets hot, rises, taking **water vapor** with it. The higher the air rises, the colder gets. Water vapo cools and chang into tiny liquid droplets, making clouds in the sky.

Environment

autumn

Deciduous woodland is an environment found in **temperate climates**, where there are four seasons every year. Closer to the equator, climates are tropical, with only two seasons.

Tropical rainforests soak up a harmful gas called carbon dioxide. **Deforestation**— when large areas of forest are cut down —means more carbon dioxide in the atmosphere. This adds to the problem of global warming.

More to explore

ducks in flight

Birds use rising currents of warm air to help them fly. Gliders and other aircraft without engines also use warm air currents to stay up in the sky.

Elephants often seek higher ground when a big storm, such as a cyclone, is on its way. Bees and other insects return to their nests, while birds fly away from the storm.

Clothes help people stay comfortable in cold and wet weather. Waterproof materials don't soak up water, so they keep people dry. Wool and fur trap air close to the skin, keeping people warm.

waterproof poncho

People who follow tornadoes to film them are called **storm chasers**. Storm chasers use information from meteorologists to find and track tornadoes.

rainbow

When light from the Sun shines through water droplets, it bends and splits into seven colors. This makes an arc of colored light, which we call a **rainbow**.

Leaves on deciduous trees change color and drop in the fall. This helps trees save energy through the winter so that they can make new leaves the next spring.

trails

The **trails** that airplanes leave behind in the sky look like clouds, but they are actually air pollution. Harmful gases in the atmosphere also lead to global warming.

Many scientists think that global warming will make **tornadoes** and other extreme storms happen more often. General weather patterns certainly alter over time —this is called climate change.

Index